Robert Pace Recital Series

SOLO ADVENTURES

By

Marion Verhaalen

Edited by Cynthia Pace

Contents

Cool Blue Cat

Marion Verhaalen

15
4
R.H: Chords may be "tossed in" freely in a jazz comp style
19
5
1
2
1
23
5
5
3
27
30
ff

In the Meadow Stood a Birch Tree

Russian Folk Song
arr. Marion Verhaalen

15
18
f
21
23
p
pp

Black is the Color of My True Love's Hair

American Folk Song
arr. Marion Verhaalen

14
18
21
25
pp
ppp

He's Gone Away

American Folk Song
arr. Marion Verhaalen

Scarborough Fair

English Folk Song
arr. Marion Verhaalen

Simply

mp p 5 mf

18
f
21
mf
25
29
p
f
33
f

37
f
41
45
mf
49
52
Rit.
p

Remembrances

Marion Verhaalen

17
21
25
29
D.C. al Coda
33
CODA
rit.
pp

Cartwheel Capers

Marion Verhaalen

28
33
L.H.
R.H.
mp
39
L.H.
R.H.
f
44
L.H.
p
48
sfz
mp
rit.